Addressing Cyber Instability

Executive Summary

Addressing Cyber Instability

Executive Summary

Cyber Conflict Studies Association

ISBN 978-1-105-54622-8

Foreword

The Cyber Conflict Studies Association (CCSA) was founded in January 2003 at an initial organizing workshop hosted by the Massachusetts Institute of Technology. The first meeting, sponsored informally by White House officials Richard Clarke and Gregory Rattray, brought together a unique blend of computer security professionals, political scientists, economists, engineers, policy wonks, and government officials. Just as nuclear scientists, social scientists, strategists, and politicians came together in an interdisciplinary fashion to address the consequences of nuclear weapons in the 1950s and 1960s, the participants agreed on the need to shape the emerging field of cyber conflict studies, providing it with intellectual heft and organizational weight.

If the creation of the CCSA in 2003 was a stake in the ground for cyber conflict as a new discipline, its published 2005 research agenda provided an initial road map for the academic and policy communities.[1] This research agenda identifies five key vectors for cyber conflict studies: international and national security, military and operational, new security agendas, legal and ethical, and methodological development. Given the embryonic state of the field in 2005, the research agenda focused on asking the right research questions rather than attempting to provide all of the answers. In subsequent years, the field's thinking has matured, but many of the research questions posited in 2005 still require more investigation and innovative thinking.

The first research category, international and national security issues, addresses the key strategic dimensions of cyber conflict, including first order concerns like the potential impact of cyber

---

[1] James Mulvenon, "Toward a Cyberconflict Studies Research Agenda," *IEEE Security and Privacy,* vol. 3, no. 4 (July/Aug 2005), 52-55, http://portal.acm.org/citation.cfm?id=1079989.

vi

attacks, especially given the fact that there is no *hard science* of cyber effects, in contrast to the rich body of work on the effects of nuclear weapons and other types of kinetic force. A second set of questions addresses the fundamental concepts of strategy, including deterrence, credibility, crisis management, and similar core concepts explored during the Cold War in the works of Thomas Schelling and others, and attempts to apply them to cyberspace. A third group of concerns delves into defensive responses to cyber threats, advocating research on how to organize in response to these issues. Lastly, this vector considers the implications for cyber conflict on inter-state relations and power dynamics based on the variety of threats, actors, and the asymmetric nature of cyber weapons.

The second category focuses on military, intelligence and operational issues, approaching cyber conflict from a military perspective. Although cyber conflict is often discussed in the media in the context of hacker attacks against Internet websites and the like, many militaries around the world devote considerable resources to exploring the use of cyber-based weapons in military conflicts with state and non-state actors. A first set of concerns examines the measurement and evaluation of cyber warfare capabilities, assessing not only technical sophistication but also cultural and organizational factors. A second group of questions involves military operational issues, such as targeting, integration with non-cyber capabilities, command and control, and human capital concerns. A final set of topics investigates dilemmas posed by military cyber defense, including attribution and international cooperation.

The third substantive research category addresses the new security challenges posed by cyberspace, since cyber conflict has proven particularly attractive to non-state or transnational actors across the entire political spectrum. The first subcategory seeks to analyze the motivations and methods of new cyber conflict actors, namely the increasing role of non-state actors. Secondly, this research vector focuses on the implications of the rise of these new cyber conflict actors for international security and the traditional national security approaches used by the U.S. and other sovereign nations.

CCSA's fourth vector, legal and ethical, investigates cyber conflict issues that are largely *terra incognita* in cyber conflict. One set of concerns relates to the legal definitions of cyber conflict and the implications of such actions in cyberspace for traditional political, social, and economic systems. A second research topic in this area catalogs the current body of domestic and international laws related to cyber conflict, assessing their applicability and sustainability in the face of technological change, and possible opportunities for refinement or replacement. The third research topic in this area focuses on the possible contributions of international, regional, and bilateral agreements and the formation of norms for governing conflict in cyberspace.

The final research vector covered by this report emphasizes the cultivation of new methodological approaches when the adaptation of traditional methodologies, i.e. those pulled from political science or strategic studies, is insufficient to comprehensively analyze cyber conflict. Our work is a combination of both old and new frameworks, since the field of cyber conflict must sample from a wide variety of methodologies and tools, ranging from the traditional to the bleeding-edge. This includes building off of traditional security approaches, for example, arms control theory, and expanding upon that foundation to best examine the most important concerns and vulnerabilities in cyber conflict.

In the six years since the publishing of the CCSA research agenda, the organization has contributed significantly to answering some of these critical questions. This monograph is an executive summary of a forthcoming book-length CCSA manuscript and represents the culmination of CCSA's work to date. It seeks to provide insights across the full spectrum of cyber conflict studies, as well as suggest avenues for follow-on research. The threat becomes more dire with each passing day; there is still a great deal of work to be done.

To contact the Cyber Conflict Studies Association:

CCSA
c/o Hannah Pitts
2650 Park Tower Drive
Suite 400
Vienna, VA 22180-7306

To contact Hannah Pitts, Executive Director, please email hannah@cyberconflict.org.

To contact James Mulvenon, Chairman of the Board, please email james@cyberconflict.org.

To contact Greg Rattray, President of CCSA, please email greg@cyberconflict.org.

Capstone: Deepening the Foundations of the Cyber Conflict Field of Study

Introduction

The emergence of cyberspace is one of the tectonic events of the 21st century. It has fundamentally altered politics, economics, social interaction, and national security, providing dramatic new opportunities, capabilities, vulnerabilities, and threats. With each passing day, cyberspace becomes an indispensible, even irreplaceable, part of the daily lives of individuals, companies, and entire nations. Yet this rapidly growing dependence on the network is bedeviled by two core problems, one technical and the other policy-related:

- *The core technical problem at the heart of cyberspace is that the underlying architecture was never designed with security in mind; indeed, the original designers never imagined that the network would be used for malicious purposes.* The priorities were, and generally remain, openness, ease of interconnection, and facilitating technical innovation. Meanwhile, the threat environment has quickly metastasized from relatively harmless webpage defacements in the mid-1990s to state-level network exploit activities, such as the Silicon Valley hacks in late 2009 and early 2010, which challenge the very heart of the American innovation economy. The vulnerabilities that make cyberspace an insecure environment and have allowed the emergence of significant malicious activity and conflict stem ultimately from a lack of priority on security in the fundamental building blocks of cyberspace. In response to these threats, we have done the best we can with an imperfect architecture, bolting security onto the network and attempting to mitigate the damage.

- *The core policy problem in cyberspace is that the evolution of the technological architecture has vastly outpaced the corresponding set of conceptual, doctrinal, organizational, and legal structures, resulting in a reactive and atavistic policy dynamic where today's ideas and organizations are often chasing yesterday's problems with no flexibility to deal with the future problems created by the introduction of yet to be invented technologies.* For national security strategists, it therefore feels like many other periods where new weapons (nuclear, chemical, biological) or modes of delivery (airplanes, ballistic missiles) were developed, and the capability was far ahead of conceptual thinking about their use and implications.

Definitions and Scope

Before delving deeper, it is first necessary to define key terms. Indeed, one of the fundamental problems over the past two decades has been deciding what to include in the definition of *cyberspace*. In the 1990s, the term was used to categorize something seen as separate and different from the physical world.[2] Over time, this point of view has evolved into viewing cyberspace as a domain, similar to land, sea, air, and space, which has in turn led to a debate about whether cyberspace can be considered a global commons.[3]

Other definitions are much less abstract, emphasizing the physical environment of cyberspace defined by its architectures and components.[4] The U.S. Department of Defense definition of

---

[2]   Gregory J. Rattray, "An Environmental Approach to Understanding Cyberpower," in *Cyberpower and National Security*, eds. Franklin D. Kramer, Stuart H. Starr, Larry K. Wentz (Dulles, VA: NDU Press, 2009), 254.

[3]   Gregory J. Rattray, Chris Evans, and Jason Healey, "American Security in the Cyber Commons," in *Contested Commons: The Future of American Power in a Multipolar World*, eds. Abraham M. Denmark and Dr. James Mulvenon (Center for a New American Security: Jan. 2010), 137-176.

[4]   Rattray, "An Environmental Approach to Understanding Cyberpower."

cyberspace, for example, emphasizes the technical infrastructure: "A global domain within the information environment consisting of the interdependent network of information technology infrastructures, including the Internet, telecommunications networks, computer systems, and embedded processors and controllers."[5] An alternative, simpler definition is that cyberspace is all interconnected information technologies.[6] The 2003 National Strategy to Secure Cyberspace calls cyberspace "the nervous system of [U.S.] critical infrastructures—the control system of our country. Cyberspace comprises hundreds of thousands of interconnected computers, servers, routers, switches, and fiber optics cables...."[7]

Whether viewed as a physical or virtual domain, it is important to note that the U.S. and other countries see cyberspace as a critical operating environment filled with complex contradictions. On the one hand, cyberspace offers dramatically exciting opportunities to unite and bind individuals and entire societies; yet on the other it simultaneously presents new, grave challenges to individual and collective security. As articulated by the recent U.S. *International Strategy for Cyberspace*: "The reach of networked technology is pervasive and global. For all nations, the underlying digital infrastructure is or will soon become a national asset."[8] As a result, it is also important to understand the dynamics and consequences of conflict within that cyberspace.

What is Cyber Conflict?

As defined in the initial CCSA research agenda in 2005, cyber conflict "is the conduct of large scale, politically motivated conflict based on the use of offensive and defensive capabilities to disrupt

---

[5] Deputy Secretary of Defense Memorandum, *Subject: The Definition of Cyberspace*, May 12, 2008.
[6] This definition is often used by Bob Gourley, one of the authors of the forthcoming CCSA volume.
[7] U.S. Executive Office of the President, *The National Strategy to Secure Cyberspace* (February 2003), 1.
[8] U.S. Executive Office of the President, *International Strategy for Cyberspace: Prosperity, Security, and Openness in a Networked World* (May 2011).

digital systems, networks, and infrastructures, including the use of cyber-based weapons or tools by non-state/transnational actors in conjunction with other forces for political ends."[9] Cyber conflict includes activities conducted by both state and non-state actors against a variety of targets. In this sense, cyber conflict is a useful term as it encompasses a number of activities that pose threats to individuals, organizations, and nation states as well as consideration with traditional military and intelligence operations. An alternative definition notes that cyber conflict is "broader than cyber warfare, including all conflicts and coercion between nations and groups for strategic purposes utilizing cyberspace where software, computers, and networks are both the means and the targets."[10] At its most basic level, cyber conflict encompasses activities conducted by many kinds of actors in order to achieve a strategic gain.

The first task of a cyber conflict studies research agenda is to refine the definition of cyber conflict itself, in particular the difficult task of categorizing formal cyber-based activity between countries (that is, cyber warfare) versus intelligence collection, covert action, crime, terrorism, and conventional war. An important, but no less difficult, categorization problem involves distinguishing between largely technology-focused research and efforts focused at the level of strategic studies. The current literature is largely divided into two different camps, with one sub-canon focused on technical issues with little concern for strategic issues and vice versa. This effort is unashamedly focused on strategic issues.

One useful distinction is to differentiate between cyber conflict and cyber crime. In a military and intelligence context, cyber conflict can largely be subsumed under a finite set of categories agreed upon by most actors, though sometimes with different names. In the U.S. Department of Defense, Computer Network Operations (CNO) includes three primary elements: Computer Network Defense (CND), Computer Network Exploitation (CNE), and Computer Network Attack (CNA). According to the revised Joint Publication 3.13 *Information Operations*:

---

[9]   Mulvenon, "Towards a Cyberconflict Studies Research Agenda," 52-55.
[10]   Jason Healey, "Advanced Intelligence Support to Cyber Conflict," Delta Risk Fundamentals for Cyber Warfare (Course Presentation, Needham, MA, September 28-30, 2010).

CNA consists of actions taken through the use of computer networks to disrupt, deny, degrade, or destroy information resident in computers and computer networks, or the computers and networks themselves. CND involves actions taken through the use of computer networks to protect, monitor, analyze, detect, and respond to unauthorized activity within DOD information systems and computer networks. CND actions not only protect DOD systems from an external adversary but also from exploitation from within, and are now a necessary function in all military operations. CNE is enabling operations and intelligence collection capabilities conducted through the use of computer networks to gather data from target or adversary automated information systems or networks.[11]

Even though we are using the definitions of the world's most powerful military, all of these CNO activities can be conducted by state actors, non-state actors, or even proxies conducting such activities on behalf of the first two. For our purposes, cyber crime does not fall within cyber conflict when the goal is commercial or direct monetary gain. For example, high-end cyber crime, including stealing vast quantities of credit card information, is not included within our definition, but cyber conflict does include *economic warfare* like embargoes, economic sabotage, or espionage to favor national defense industries.

We do not directly address issues related to the *soft* side of information-gathering operations, such as perception management (actions to convey or deny selected information, and indicators to influence emotions, motives, and objective reasoning), deception (measures designed to mislead the enemy by manipulation, distortion, or falsification of evidence to induce a reaction), and other psychological operations (activities to convey selected information and indicators to foreign audiences to influence their emotions, motives, objective reasoning, and ultimately the behavior of foreign governments, organizations, groups, and individuals). These are generally considered *information operations* (IO) or military

---

[11]   U.S. Joint Staff, *Information Operations*, Joint Publication 3.13 (February, 13 2006).

information support operations (MISO), in United States military parlance. The broader IO construct does include CNO, and cyberspace will be an essential medium for the conduct of the other aspects of IO.

The strategic implications of cyber conflict also reach far beyond the military, intelligence, and economic sectors—extending into realm of diplomacy and statecraft. As states increasingly recognize the utility of cyberspace as a tool of national security, it is necessary to examine the implications of cyber conflict for bilateral and multilateral relations, civil society, and international legal regimes. Allegations of cross-border hacking, whether the cyber operation is classified as an attack or as espionage, have a profound effect on both official and unofficial channels of diplomacy. Additional diplomatic ramifications of cyber conflict include the recent increased attention to the problems of Internet freedom, [12] soft power, [13] the role of cyberspace in uprisings around the world, and the release of classified data on a major scale. [14] All of these phenomena complicate the roles and responsibility for the world's leaders. As summarized by Nye, "States will remain the dominant actor on the world stage, but they will find the stage far more crowded and difficult to control."[15] As such, the entry costs decline and "world politics will not be the sole province of governments."[16]

---

[12] See Executive Office of the President, *International Strategy of Cyberspace.* Evgeny Morozov, *The Net Delusion: The Dark Side of Internet Freedom* (New York: PublicAffairs, 2011); Hillary Clinton, "Remarks on Internet Freedom," Remarks at the Newseum, January, 21 2010; Hillary Clinton, "Internet Rights and Wrongs: Choices and Challenges in a Networked World," Remarks at George Washington University, February 15, 2011.

[13] See, for example, Joseph S. Nye, Jr., *The Future of Power* (New York: PublicAffairs, 2011); Ed. Leigh Armistead, *Information Operations: Warfare and the Hard Reality of Soft Power* (Dulles, VA: Brassey's, 2004); Joseph S. Nye, Jr., "The Information Revolution and American Soft Power," *Asia-Pacific Review*, vol. 1, no. 1 (2002); Shanthi Kalathil, "China's Soft Power in the Information Age: Think Again," ISD Working Papers (New Diplomacy, May 2011).

[14] John Markoff, "The Asymmetrical Online War," Bits Blog, *New York Times*, April 3, 2011, http://bits.blogs.nytimes.com/2011/04/03/the-asymmetrical-online-war.

[15] Nye, *The Future of Power*, 116.
[16] Ibid.

Beyond the strategic implications of cyberspace, its profound impact on societal developments is apparent. The Internet and cyberspace decentralizes communication and information, increasing capacity, speed, and directness. [17] Social media and other communications media, including Facebook, Twitter, blogs, and messaging, are reshaping how individuals relate to information and each other. Decentralized networks of information can proliferate with relative ease and speed. Chatting online with a friend in Tokyo is as easy as if she were sitting a few city blocks away. While not all developments in cyberspace are positive, it has already expanded the global commons and increased our ability to communicate more easily and more quickly. We can see the effects of this social interaction in the uprisings of the so-called "Arab Spring" across North Africa and the Middle East, but these same examples also demonstrate the continued roles of states to use information technology against its citizens and disrupt social development. [18] While these issues are not a major focus of this monograph, they are increasingly the fundamental concerns of leaders around the globe that will impact the relative openness of cyberspace as well as other features that will shape the cyber conflict environment.

The Threat Environment

Even as the world becomes more dependent on cyberspace in every facet of life, the threat environment has become more dire, driven by both fundamental flaws in the underlying architecture and the desire to prioritize connectivity over security. The spectrum of cyber threats ranges widely, from lower level threats like defacements to intermediate threats like botnets and malware, to a new threshold of cyber attacks established by the Stuxnet worm. [19] Not only is the spectrum of threats wide in breadth, but

---

[17]   Ibid.
[18]   For the canonical articulation of this argument, see Morozov, *The Net Delusion*. See also, for example, James Cowie, "Egypt Leaves the Internet," *Renesys* (blog), January 27, 2011, http://www.renesys.com/blog/2011/01/egypt-leaves-the-internet.shtml.
[19]   William J. Broad and David E. Danger, "Worm Was Perfect for Sabotaging Centrifuges," *New York Times*, November 18, 2010,

the potential actors and adversaries are proliferating at the speed of the network. States and non-state actors, including state-sponsored organizations or proxies, have varying levels of capability and intent but still comprise a significant level of threat in cyberspace. Increasing dependence on cyberspace across all dimensions of national power (political, economic, military, diplomatic, and social) only increases vulnerabilities and the potential negative consequences of not adequately understanding the threats.

While Stuxnet is considered the new pinnacle of cyber threats, cyber espionage, not cyber attack or cyber war, is currently the most pressing risk for the United States in cyberspace. Strategic espionage against political, military, and intelligence targets can change the outcome of interstate conflicts and even alter the balance of power, while economic espionage can result in substantial economic losses and can endanger future competitive advantage.[20] Within the espionage realm, Advanced Persistent Threat poses the most significant, sustained challenge to actors in cyberspace. Advanced Persistent Threat, or APT, consists of highly sophisticated intrusion activities, best documented in efforts targeted at the U.S. Government or companies in the Defense Industrial Base (DIB) but expanding to include companies at the core of the innovation economy such as Google.[21] Threats against the DIB and the government are only compounded by serious and

---

http://www.nytimes.com/2010/11/19/world/middleeast/19stuxnet.html. For more information on Stuxnet, see Ralph Langner, "Cracking Stuxnet, a 21st-century cyber weapon," *TED* (March 2011) http://www.ted.com/talks/ralph_langner_cracking_stuxnet_a_21st_century_c yberweapon.html?awesm=on.ted.com_Langner&utm_content=awesm-publisher&utm_medium=on.ted.com-static&utm_source=langner.com.

[20] Nye, *The Future of Power*, 145. For a specific example of cyber espionage, see Brian Grow and Mark Hosenball, "Special Report: In cyberspy vs. cyberspy, China has the edge," *Reuters*, April 14, 2011, http://www.reuters.com/article/2011/04/14/us-china-usa-cyberespionage-idUSTRE73D24220110414.

[21] "Under Cyberthreat: Defense Contractors," *Businessweek*, July 6, 2009, http://www.businessweek.com/technology/content/jul2009/tc2009076_8735 12.htm. See also, Brian Grow, Keith Epstein and Chi-Chu Tschang, "The New E-spionage Threat," *Businessweek*, April 10, 2008, http://www.businessweek.com/magazine/content/08_16/b4080032218430.ht m.

known vulnerabilities in critical infrastructure, which are often privately held but are crucial for government services.

Another important class of threats against states include activities designed to deny access to cyber resources, such as the Distributed Denial of Service attacks (DDoS) against Estonia in 2007, which took down the websites of many Estonian organizations, including the parliament, banks, and media following increased tensions with Russia. The Estonian disruption also included defacements and other lower level methods, although the DDoS attacks caused the most significant, sustained damage. While some Russian hackers have taken responsibility for the attacks, no official connection with the Russian government has been uncovered. The Estonian experience was repeated during the 2008 cyber disruptions before and during the brief war between Georgia and Russia, including defacement and DDoS attacks against Georgian government and media websites, again presumably by Russian-backed actors.

Taken together, these various classes of cyber threats present a significant threat to the viability of cyberspace as a useable domain by states, groups, or individuals, necessitating a systematic examination of the dynamics of cyber conflict.

The Evolution of Cyber Thinking

Cyber conflict studies, though embryonic, represent an attempt to comprehensively identify and analyze the origins, modes, and possible consequences of conflict in cyberspace, fusing together a wide range of interdisciplinary approaches. Though the field of cyber conflict studies has clearly matured over time, it has not kept pace with the rapid technological developments that have accelerated the evolution of this type of conflict. This section provides an overview of the state of the field before the establishment of the CCSA and how it has evolved through the years. It is not intended to be a literature review of cyber conflict studies, as more detailed overviews of existing scholarship are included in the relevant chapters.

Since the creation of the foundational technologies themselves, decades of books, monographs, think-tank studies, presidential commissions, and industry reports have contributed to the body of cyber conflict knowledge. Many of these writings have not stood the test of time, overcome by events or rendered obsolete by the advance of technology. In general, they all share a deep concern about the vulnerabilities of the network, and, to a lesser extent, they have offered possible solutions. As global dependencies on the network proliferate, writings have increasingly warned of the potential for strategic cyber attacks, including the potential of a catastrophic cyber attack against the United States. Others have warned about the theft of money and intellectual property through cyber attack. Yet very little of this literature could be considered a contribution to a field, since the articles rarely referenced each other and therefore were not building systematized knowledge. With so many issues to explore and policies to establish or optimize, cyber conflict research needs to a more cumulative approach, and the following survey is meant to capture this foundation of cyber conflict research to date.

Although the network was born in the 1960s with the work of Paul Baran and the initial ARPANET projects, cyber conflict did not become an issue of concern until the late 1980s, when two significant events raised concerns about the security and reliability of the Internet.[22] In 1987, researcher Cliff Stoll uncovered a hacker using the Lawrence Berkeley National Laboratory Network to hack into other networks, including military bases and defense contractors.[23] One year later, Robert Morris, Cornell University graduate student and the son of an NSA scientist, unleashed the first worm into the Internet. He was convicted under the 1986 Computer Fraud and Abuse Act, although Morris stated that he wrote the worm to measure the size of the Internet and his stated intent was not malicious.[24] As a result of the Morris Worm, the CERT/CC was established, beginning the evolution of offense-defense interactions that continues to this day.[25]

The early literature was also marked by a series of prescient theorizing that, in retrospect, had a clear view of the coming cyber conflict environment. In their series of books, including *Future Shock*

---

[22]   Katie Hafner, *Where Wizards Stay Up Late: The Origins of the Internet* (New York: Simon & Schuster, 1998).

[23]   Cliff Stoll, *The Cuckoo's Egg* (New York: Gallery Books, 2005).

[24]   Ted Eisenberg et al., "The Cornell Commission: On Morris and the Worm," *Communications of the ACM*, vol. 32, no. 6 (June 1989).

[25]   Hilarie Orman, "The Morris Worm: A Fifteen-Year Perspective," *IEEE Security & Privacy,* vol. 1, no. 5 (September/October 2003): 35-43.

(1970), *The Third Wave* (1984), and *War and Anti-War* (1993), futurists Alvin and Heidi Toffler unveiled a vision for an Information Age built on information and communication technologies that would overturn the status quo of nation-state power and precipitate "the deepest social upheaval and creative restructuring of all times."[26] The Tofflers also understood that these new technologies would empower non-state groups in more violent ways as well: "The Second Wave [Industrial Age] idea that national governments are the only ones that can wield military force is now obsolete."[27] In their view, small groups in the future would be able to militarily challenge states and societies with the nuclear material and knowledge streaming out of the then-destitute former Soviet Union, with portable biological labs, and, yes, with cyber attacks. Other early important theoretical contributions were offered by John Arquilla and David Ronfeldt, whose *Networks and Netwars* (2001), *In Athena's Camp* (1997), and *Cyberwar is Coming!* (1993) offer some of the most innovative and cross-disciplinary analyses of the subject to date, especially through their application of network theory to cyber conflict.[28][29][30] Arquilla and Ronfeldt added early clarification to what was meant by *cyber war*, which they defined as "conducting, and preparing to conduct, military operations according to information-related principles."[31] Finally, cyber gadflies like Winn Schwartau in his 1994 book *Information Warfare* offered the first examination of the construct of information warfare.[32]

In the early 1990s, the policy community began to systematically explore the early symptoms of cyber conflict. In 1991, the National Research Council produced "Computers at

---

[26]   Alvin and Heidi Toffler, *The Third Wave* (New York, NY: Bantam, 1984), 10.
[27]   Toffler, *War and Anti-War* (New York, NY: Grand Central Publishing,1993), 270.
[28]   John Arquilla and David Ronfeldt, *Networks and Netwars: The Future of Terror, Crime, and Militancy* (Santa Monica, CA: RAND, 2001).
[29]   John Arquilla and David Ronfeldt, *In Athena's camp: Preparing for Conflict in the Information Age* (Santa Monica, CA: RAND, 1997).
[30]   Arquilla and Ronfeldt, "Cyberwar is coming!" *Comparative Strategy,* vol. 12, no. 2 (1993): 141-165.
[31]   Ibid., 144.
[32]   Winn Schwartau, *Information Warfare* (New York, NY: Thunder's Mouth Press, 1994).

Risk," a still relevant articulation of the importance of security in the face of advanced threats.[33] "Computers at Risk" also addressed the importance of non-state actors in information security, describing the "high-grade threat" in perhaps the first unclassified description of what is today called the Advanced Persistent Threat.[34] Significant policy contributions in the 1990s were also made by Roger Molander and Peter Wilson, whose monograph *Strategic Information Warfare Rising* attempted to formulate a common Department of Defense strategy and policy framework for addressing the challenge of strategic information warfare.[35]

Researchers of this period also articulated clear, compelling rational for enhancing our ability to defend systems. In 1995, Bruce Berkowitz wrote that cyber attacks could degrade both civilian and military networks, emphasizing the importance of mounting an information warfare *civil defense*: "Civilian information systems are prime candidates for attack.... Just as cities are targeted in strategic bombing, in future wars we can expect civilian information systems to be hacked, tapped, penetrated, bugged, and infected with computer viruses."[36] In 1996, a RAND team that included Roger Molander clearly laid out the vulnerabilities and stakes involved: "Civilian data encryption and system protection are rudimentary. Talented computer hackers in distant countries may be able to gain access to large portions of the information infrastructure underlying both U.S. economic well being and defense logistics and communications."[37] At a more general level, Dorothy Denning's *Information Warfare and Security* provides a comprehensive and detailed look at three categories of information warfare: computer crime, cybercrime, and information terrorism.[38] It discusses government use of information

---

[33] National Research Council, *Computers at Risk: Safe Computing in the Information Age* (Washington, DC: National Academies Press, 1991).

[34] Ibid., 283-285.

[35] Roger C. Molander, *Strategic Information Warfare Rising* (Santa Monica, CA: RAND, 1998).

[36] Bruce Berkowitz, "Warfare in the Information Age," *Issues in Science and Technology*, (University of Texas at Dallas, 1995), 59-66.

[37] Gregory J. Rattray, *Strategic Warfare in Cyberspace* (Cambridge, MA: The MIT Press, 2001).

[38] Dorothy Denning, *Information Warfare and Security*, (New York: Addison-Wesley Professional, 1998).

warfare for law enforcement investigations and for military and intelligence operations, conflicts arising in the areas of free speech and encryption, offensive information warfare, deceptive exploitation of information, denial of access to information, and defensive information warfare, especially information security principles and practices.

By the mid 1990s, the U.S. government had recognized the growing problem of cyber conflict and its various departments began to tackle key aspects of the issue. The Defense Science Board (DSB) issued two important reports on cyber conflict, particularly their 1996 report "Information Warfare (Defense)" and their 2000 report "Defensive Information Operations," placing an important official DoD stamp on what was still an insurgent doctrinal movement. Other parts of the government, especially the White House staff under the leadership of CCSA initiator Richard Clarke, recognized that the nation had become increasingly reliant on civilian infrastructures, not just for the Internet and communications, but also on the electrical and financial industries. These themes of threat, vulnerability, dependence, and cooperation were first introduced in the President's Commission on Critical Infrastructure Protection (PCCIP) (1997). The PCCIP report, a product of a fifteen-month effort, focused on requirements for ensuring the security, continuity, and availability of critical infrastructures.[39] The commission was widely credited for highlighting the fact that all infrastructures share a collective dependence on information and communication capabilities, calling for enhanced means to protect the nation from cyber threats. Many of the structures for information sharing and analysis in place today were established based on this report's recommendations, and it remains a key reference for cyber studies.

At the same time that the government was paying greater attention to cyber conflict issues, the academic literature on the topic matured significantly, bringing methodological rigor and interdisciplinary breadth. Gregory Rattray's 2001 *Strategic Warfare in Cyberspace* was the first comprehensive treatment of cyber conflict that placed the phenomena within the terminological and theoretical

---

[39] *Critical Foundations: Protecting America's Infrastructures,* The Report of the President's Commission on Critical Infrastructure Protection (October 1997).

constructs of the strategic literature, establishing a framework for examining the dynamics of warfare in the emerging cyberspace environment.[40] The book examines the nature of the cyberspace environment, the potential for disruptive action in cyberspace, and the dynamics of cyber conflict. The work compares cyber with other forms of strategic warfare, such as nuclear, strategic air strikes, and naval blockades, and then applies the frameworks for successful conduct of strategic offense and defense to the realm of cyber conflict. The growing maturity of the cyber conflict field was also marked by the arrival of articulate skeptics of prevailing assumptions and shibboleths. Martin Libicki's 1997 monograph, *Defending Cyberspace and Other Metaphors*,[41] incisively questions many of the core assumptions of the cyber warfare literature. His 2007 work, *Conquest in Cyberspace: National Security and Information Warfare*, argues that the possibilities of hostile attacks are less threatening than mainstream analysts assert, and his 2009 book, *Cyberdeterrence and Cyberwar*, raises serious questions about the applicability of strategic theory to cyber conflict.[42]

After 9/11, the world naturally focused on counter-terrorism but the rapidly evolving and growing threats in cyberspace did not give policymakers the luxury of only focusing on kinetic terrorism. Then-Director of National Intelligence Mike McConnell's stark warning to President George W. Bush that a cyber attack against Wall Street could produce more economic damage than 9/11 led the Administration to promulgate the *National Strategy to Secure Cyberspace* (2003), Homeland Security Presidential Directive 7 (2003), and the Comprehensive National Cybersecurity Initiative at the end of the Administration.

Since the end of the Bush Administration, largely as a function of the growing realization of the scale of APT and its potential damage to U.S. national power, the policy community has arguably seized upon cyber conflict as one of the top national security threats. In the run-up

---

[40]   Rattray, *Strategic Warfare in Cyberspace.*
[41]   Martin C. Libicki, *Defending Cyberspace and Other Metaphors,* (Washington, DC: U.S. Government Printing Office, 1997).
[42]   Martin Libicki, *Conquest in Cyberspace: National Security and Information Warfare,* (New York, NY: Cambridge University Press, 2007); Martin Libicki, *Cyberdeterrence and Cyberwar*, (Santa Monica, CA: RAND Corporation, 2009).

to the 2008 presidential election, the CSIS Commission on Cybersecurity for the 44th Presidency published "Securing Cyberspace for the 44th Presidency."[43] This report focused on issues beyond the scope of cyber conflict, but emphasized the importance of cyber security for U.S. domestic and international policy. Following the *60-Day Cyber Review* in 2009, President Obama encapsulated many of these lessons in a major speech on cyber policy, which eventually resulted in the creation of the White House *cyber czar* position.

After the issuance of the White House strategy, national institutions published three significant cyber publications. In 2009, the National Research Council published *Technology, Policy, Law, and Ethics Regarding U.S. Acquisition and Use of Cyberattack Capabilities*, edited by William Owens, Kenneth Dam, and Herbert Lin.[44] This first major review of how the U.S. acquires and might use cyber attack capabilities provides an excellent overall description of the cyber environment and how it enables asymmetric attacks but is limited in its treatment of non-state actors. The National Defense University's 2009 edited volume *Cyberpower and National Security* provided a significant baselining of current military-associated academic thought regarding cyber conflict.[45] Chapters covered a wide range of topics, including technology issues, military operations, crime, Internet governance, law, and critical infrastructure protection. In his policy recommendations, Franklin Kramer, continues a plea echoed for the last two decades: "Since cyber conflict and cyber power is a fundamental fact of global life, the United States must create an effective national and international strategic framework for the development and use of cyber conflict as part of an overall national security strategy." In their 2010 study *Proceedings of a Workshop on Deterring Cyberattacks: Informing Strategies and Developing Options*, the National Research Council emphasized the problem of offense, examining how, for example, attribution might be

---

[43]   Center for Strategic and International Studies, *Securing Cyberspace for the 44th President: A Report on Cybersecurity for the 44th President* (December 2008).

[44]   William A. Owens, Kenneth W. Dam, and Herbert S. Lin, eds., *Technology, Policy, Law, and Ethics Regarding U.S. Acquisition and Use of Cyberattack Capabilities* (Washington, DC: National Academies Press, 2009).

[45]   Franklin D. Kramer, Stuart H. Starr, and Larry Wentz, *Cyberpower and National Security* (Dulles, VA: Potomac Books, Inc., 2009).

improved to better deter non-state actors. Looking at challenges of attribution, strategy policy and doctrine, deterrence concepts, and law and regulation broadly, this workshop and the associated volume of research put forward a very cohesive body of research into the social and political aspects of cyber conflict from a nation-state perspective.

Perhaps the best evidence of the emerging centrality of cyber issues in the national security policy debate is the fact that the subject has been integrated into the writings of senior national security strategists. Richard Clarke and Robert Knake's *Cyber War* traces earlier examples of cyber conflict and proposes domestic and international solutions for improving global cyber security.[46] The book also criticizes current U.S. policy and argues that even though the U.S. pioneered the Internet and cyberspace, it is being left behind by new developments and imperiled by new threats. Similarly, Joseph Nye discusses cyberspace and international security dynamics in his new magnum opus, *The Future of Power*.[47] The primary contribution of Nye's book is that it takes cyber conflict out of its usual self-referential mode and places it within the larger context of national security concerns for the United States and the international system.

The latest emerging theme in the cyber conflict literature highlights the reassertion of governments in cyberspace. In the early days of the Internet, self-described prophets like John Perry Barlow told governments that cyberspace was "naturally independent of the tyrannies you seek to impose on us." While it remains generally true that "governance in cyberspace resembles the American Wild West … with limited governmental authority and engagement," [48] governments have increasingly been able to reassert their dominance in the cyber domain, just as they do in the air, sea, space, and maritime domains. Re-assertion of government sovereignty in cyberspace, while driven by every nation's increasing dependence on the network for prosperity and security, also derives from the realization that every switch, every router, every node in the network lies within the boundaries of a sovereign nation-state or travels over

---

[46]   Richard A. Clarke and Robert K. Knake *Cyber War* (New York: Ecco, 2010).

[47]   Nye, *The Future of Power*.

[48]   Eds. Abe Denmark and James Mulvenon, *Contested Commons: The Future of American Power in a Multipolar World*, Center for a New American Security.

cable or satellite owned by a company governed by the laws of a sovereign nation-state. Authoritarian regimes, such as China, Saudi Arabia, or Iran, have been quicker to operationalize this revelation for the benefit of the state. Jack Goldsmith and Tim Wu wrote convincingly in *Who Controls the Internet* that nations were imposing borders into cyberspace to control content, whether it was China blocking content that criticized the regime or France blocking the sale of Nazi memorabilia in online auctions.[49] More recently, Evgeny Morozov argued in *The Net Delusion* that the "idea that the Internet favors the oppressed rather than the oppressor is marred by ... a naïve belief in the emancipatory nature of online communication."[50] The recent, near total shutdown of the Egyptian Internet will surely generate more significant research both into the government control of the Internet—as well as whether such control will be effective.[51]

Current State of the CCSA Research Vectors

CCSA's forthcoming book-length manuscript, the product of a two-year study, brings together leading thinkers in the field to address each of the five major research vectors (international and national security, military and operational, new security agendas, legal and ethical, and methodological development). The following sections are a summary of the manuscript's findings.

Vector One: Strategic-Level Issues

The emergence of cyber conflict is a key strategic challenge of the twenty-first century, adding to the ongoing dilemmas posed by nuclear warfare and terrorism. When examining the core strategic issues posed by cyber conflict, one must first begin with

---

[49] Jack Goldsmith and Tim Wu, *Who Controls the Internet? Illusions of a Borderless World* (New York: Oxford University Press, 2006).

[50] Morozov, *The Net Delusion*, xiii.

[51] See the excellent blogs from Renesys which tracked these developments as they happened: James Cowie, "Egypt Leaves the Internet," January 27, 2011, http://www.renesys.com/blog/2011/01/egypt-leaves-the-internet.shtml and James Cowie, "Egypt Returns to the Internet," February 2, 2011, http http://www.renesys.com/blog/2011/02/egypt-returns-to-the-internet.shtml.

definitional problems and progressing through the core elements of the historical canon, exploring the cyber dimensions of concepts such as deterrence, compellence, escalation control, command and control, and war termination. While inspired by the works of Kahn, Wohlstetter, Schelling, Ellsberg, et al., one must also explicitly delineate the fundamental similarities and differences with the nuclear analogy, building a conceptual structure that does not simply attempt to pound a square cyber peg into a round nuclear hole. What, then, are the key similarities and differences between cyber conflict and nuclear warfare?

Table 1.1: Key Similarities Between Cyber and Nuclear Conflict

1.   Both operate at all three levels of military operations: strategic,[52] operational, and tactical, with the potential to have effects ranging from small- to population-scale.

2.   Both have the capacity to create large-scale, even existentially, destructive effects.

3.   Both can be conducted between nation-states, between a nation-state and non-state-actors, or between hybrids involving nation-states and non-state-actor proxies.

4.   Both nuclear and cyber conflict "could present the adversary with decisive defeat, negating the need to fight conventional wars."[53]

5.   Both can intentionally or unintentionally cause *cascade effects* beyond the scope of the original attack target.

Table 1.2: Key Differences Between Cyber and Nuclear Conflict

1.   Attribution of the attacker was never a problem in the mature phases of nuclear conflict, thanks to technologies like the DEW line and the DSP constellation, but it is the *central* problem in cyber conflict.

---

[52]   The term "strategic" is defined here to mean warfare designed to "defeat opponents through attacks on centers of gravity without fighting fielded forces." See Rattray, *Strategic Warfare in Cyberspace*, 20.

[53]   Ibid.

2. The medium for cyber conflict is man-made, largely in private sector hands, and would likely traverse infrastructure of non-combatants, while the medium for nuclear conflict includes only sovereign domains (nation's airspace, land, and coastal waters) and the global commons (airspace, sea, and space).

3. Low cost and ease of availability means that millions of people around the world have potential access to potent cyber attack tools, whereas access to operational nuclear weapons has been historically limited to a small number of nation-states with sufficient resources to build them.

4. Whereas nuclear warfare can only be conducted in a violent way, cyber conflict can be conducted in "either a physically violent or nonviolent way," creating both physical destruction (e.g., "blanking the screen of air traffic controllers so that airliners crash") as well as virtual destruction (e.g., deleting data).[54]

5. Computer network attack can be conducted covertly, whereas the dramatic, overt effects of nuclear attack make covertness impossible.

6. Use of nuclear weapons is unambiguously viewed as an act of aggression justifying retaliation, whereas significant ambiguities continue to bedevil attempts to define clear legal and ethical boundaries in cyber conflict.

7. Offensive and defensive weapons are easier to distinguish in nuclear combat, while "the tools and techniques used to conduct digital warfare are often useful to both attackers and defenders."[55]

8. Cyber attack and defense tools have significant dual-use applications, whereas there are no appreciable dual-use applications for nuclear weapons.

9. Whereas the effects of nuclear weapons can be scientifically delineated from the laws of physics (see *Effects of Nuclear Weapons*), cyber attacks are much more uncertain.

---

[54] Ibid., 19.
[55] Ibid., 135.

10. Since U.S. government and military networks are scanned and pinged every second, *thresholds* is a much more difficult problem for retaliation and escalation to cyber attack than the "acknowledged threshold" of nuclear attack.[56]

11. In nuclear war, "the 1000th bomb could be as powerful as the first," whereas in cyber the second attack could be thwarted by the results of the first.[57]

12. In nuclear conflict, counterforce has been possible, but there are real questions as to whether you can really attack a nation's offensive cyber capabilities.[58]

13. In nuclear war, one has not worried about the intervention of third parties, but third parties are likely to get involved in cyber conflict whether the primary participants want them to or not.[59]

14. Private firms have not been expected to defend themselves in nuclear war, whereas they are responsible for their own defense in cyber conflict.[60]

15. Finally, no higher level of war has existed in nuclear conflict, whereas cyber can always escalate to nuclear war.[61]

The differences listed in this table cannot be dismissed as minor, since some strike at the very heart of core dynamics of nuclear conflict. But the terminology and conceptual vocabulary of the canon remain a critical resource for understanding cyber conflict, once they are modified to accommodate cyber's different technological characteristics and modalities.

With the nuclear analogy properly scoped, the discussion naturally turns to the core issue of deterrence. While the United States wisely retains the intention and capability to initiate cyber conflict at a time and place of its own choosing, it naturally seeks to deter other adversaries from the same goal, particularly given

---

[56] Libicki, *Cyberdeterrence and Cyberwar*, xvi.
[57] Ibid.
[58] Ibid.
[59] Ibid.
[60] Ibid.
[61] Ibid.

the asymmetric dependence of the United States on cyberspace for economic, political, and technological power. While it is well-known that US government, military, and corporate networks have been the target of sustained computer network exploit activities over the last ten years, it must be noted that the country has not yet been the target of the type of large-scale computer network attack envisioned by Richard Clarke and others in their writings. How can we explain this apparent gap? Why have adversaries not taken advantage of clear vulnerabilities to launch cyber attacks against the United States? Have they not developed sufficient capabilities to do so? This is hard to believe given the sophistication of the intrusion sets. Has there not yet been the right combination of strategic circumstance and perceived payoff, such as the China-Taiwan contingency involving US military intervention discussed later in the chapter, to justify using known capabilities? Or, despite its strategic confusion, does the United States currently enjoy a form of tacit cyber deterrence from computer network attack, and if so, what is the basis for this tacit deterrence?

When unpacking cyber deterrence, the canon typologizes deterrence into two categories: deterrence through denial and deterrence through punishment. Cyber deterrence through denial is also primarily based on computer network defense. One piece of good news is that the *attribution problem*, which occupies center stage in the discussion of the dilemmas posed by cyber deterrence by punishment, is not as significant an issue in cyber deterrence by denial, because it is not critical to know who might attack, only whether you are vulnerable to attack. Also, two primary methods for protecting retaliatory forces are mobility and concealment.[62] Cyber forces, by virtue of their form factor, (i.e., a laptop is easier to conceal than a ballistic missile submarine) are already more mobile and more concealed than nuclear forces ever were. Finally, the inability to disarm an adversary's cyber attack capability has three benefits: (1) reduced incentives for preemption; (2) retaliation can be more focused and proportional; and (3) reduced demand for immediate retaliation ("use it or lose it").[63]

---

[62] Thomas C. Schelling, *The Strategy of Conflict* (Cambridge, MA: Harvard University Press, 1981), 243.

[63] Libicki, *Cyberdeterrence and Cyberwar*, 61-62.

But the cyber offense-defense balance is a huge problem for cyber deterrence by denial. As discussed earlier, fundamental security was not built into the architecture design of cyberspace, and we have been gluing security onto the side of the network ever since. Without fundamental re-architecting of the network, which is unlikely in the short-term, is deterrence by denial even possible? In the short-term, Rattray argues that these defensive dilemmas put a greater onus on risk management than impenetrable protection: "Diffuse vulnerabilities and limited resources also require defensive efforts predicated on managing the risks of attacks rather than establishing comprehensive defenses capable of assured protection." [64] But Owens, et al., write, "the gap between the attacker's capability to attack many vulnerable targets and the defender's inability to defend all of them is growing rather than diminishing." [65] In addition, cyber offensive capabilities are dramatically cheaper than effective cyber defensive capabilities. As is often pointed out, the cyber warrior, armed perhaps with a minimal kit (computer, Internet connection, and publicly available tools) only needs to find one way in, but the cyber defender, protecting perhaps a huge network of thousands of heterogeneous nodes with dozens of access points, needs to stop every possible avenue of approach. Thus, deterrence by denial in cyber is also cost-prohibitive. For both of these reasons, it appears that cyber deterrence by denial may be less credible than deterrence by punishment, which likely has a much higher chance of success.

In the cyber realm, deterrence by punishment theoretically offers better chances of success, especially against adversaries that have well-developed cyber infrastructure. As Owens, et al., argue, "Deterrence by punishment is more likely to be an effective strategy against nations that are highly dependent on information technology, because such nations have a much larger number of potential targets that can be attacked. Nevertheless, even nations with a less technologically sophisticated national infrastructure are probably vulnerable to cyberattack in selected niches." [66] Moreover, the will to retaliate is arguably less of a factor in cyber

---

[64]   Rattray, *Strategic Warfare in Cyberspace*, 474.
[65]   Owens, Dam, and Lin, eds., *Cyberattack Capabilities*, 44.
[66]   Ibid., 41.

attack than nukes, given its plausible deniability, potentially covert nature, and less physically destructive effects.[67]

Yet cyber deterrence through punishment is also highly problematic. The main challenges for cyber deterrence through punishment are: (1) the so-called *attribution problem*, which makes it difficult to identify the attacker in the first place; and (2) a series of credibility problems, including automaticity of response, unavailability of retaliatory targets, demonstration of effect, uncertainty of cyber effects, repeatability of effect, survivability of retaliatory capability, thresholds, signaling, command and control, and extended deterrence. None of these challenges can be solved alone through policy measures like stated declaratory policies. All of these challenges create strategic instability in cyber conflict, and undermine the utility of deterrence through punishment.

Our research leads us to the stark conclusion that the cyberspace domain is inherently unstable, and teases out the strategic implications of that finding. The current strategic cyber environment is marked by an inability to establish credible deterrence and effectively prevent the emergence of adversaries and conflicts in cyberspace detrimental to U.S. interests. The sources of this instability are many-fold. First, the technical architecture undergirding cyberspace is highly permissive of cyber intrusions and attacks, resulting in a system that is extremely hard to defend and confers dominance to the offense. The defender can mitigate the asymmetry by reducing the degree of interconnectivity, or even disconnecting networks, but this move is very costly given the growing reliance of the United States and advanced nations on these networks for a wide range of economic activity and military operations. Second, the design of the architecture often provides the attacker with anonymity and plausible deniability, exacerbated by the lack of effective governance of the network focused on mitigating malicious activity. Third, the relatively low cost of technology and operations significantly lowers the barriers to entry for the attacker, enabling a wide range of actors to acquire capabilities. Fourth, cyber operations running at the rapid speed of the network deny defenders and the political leadership sufficient time for assessment and decision-making. Automation may mitigate this problem, but the risks are both

---

[67]   Libicki, *Cyberdeterrence and Cyberwar*, 69-71.

high and unknown. Fifth, the pace of technological change and the breadth of network connectivity are outpacing both defensive approaches at the enterprise or engineering level as well as the policy and legal constructs promulgated to guide their operations.

Moreover, these conditions are only getting worse with the proliferation of social media, mobile communications, and the migration to cloud computing. The Internet underground capable of exploiting these trends is alive and well, with pirates and mercenaries thriving in a swampy ecosystem that makes hiding and attacking too easy. And lastly, while the issues are acknowledged, little progress is being made in terms of improving security and resilience as a key aspect of Internet governance. The implications of this conclusion are explored in the final section of the monograph.

Vector Two: Military and Operational

Cyber conflict must also be examined at the operational level, focusing particularly on how military and intelligence strategy, doctrine, and organizations have evolved in the United States, culminating in the formation of a Cyber Command (CYBERCOM). While CYBERCOM has provided a coherent construct for the organization of U.S. military cyber operations it has also resulted in the perception that the U.S. seeks to militarize and dominate cyberspace. There are continuing strains between the cyber-related activities and roles of the military on the one hand and the intelligence community on the other, which is complicated by the increasing use of cyber capabilities to further intelligence collection and constraints posed by current domestic legal frameworks to effectively integrate such operations.

Given the nature of the cyber environment, what sort of military and intelligence organizations or capabilities are needed? As a first principle, bureaucracies and people in this environment must develop new capabilities to adapt to new threats in a fast and agile way. Second, military cyber defense must be increasingly collaborative with other actors, including non-governmental organizations, researchers, corporations, and other groups outside traditional national security communities. This collaboration must be focused on developing resilience in the face of a continuously evolving threat that has demonstrated that it *will* penetrate defenses. Third, those combating cyber threats must ensure that they maintain sufficient knowledge capture to build upon existing experience and lessons. Current U.S. military and intelligence approaches must demonstrate significant continued evolution in light of the challenges posed by strategic instability, with a focus on removing policy and operational barriers to defensive collaboration and avoiding generating perceptions of the U.S. as a source of threats and instability in cyberspace.

Vector Three: Non-State Actors in Cyberspace

Current CCSA research on the *new security agenda* sector focuses on the role of non-state actors in cyber conflict and the challenges of managing conflicts that will necessarily involve much greater roles for non-state actors. By highlighting the common misperception regarding the dominance of state actors in the dynamics of conflict in cyberspace, CCSA is focused instead on developing new thinking about cyber conflict management and mitigation, emphasizing the current and potential role of non-states. CCSA research covers substantial ground in considering the new roles for non-state actors and their implications on traditional and new security considerations. For example, research must directly address the potential emergence of significant cyber threats based on non-state actors conducting guerilla campaigns against economic and social centers of gravity, along with the limitations of traditional national security and law enforcement approaches in addressing such threats. There is a pressing need to develop mechanisms to foster defensive collaboration as a means to more effectively address concerns of cyber instability that involves a wide range of non-state actors—network operators, vendors, security researchers, CERTs, and other operational responders. Such collaboration will prove an essential aspect of both national security-focused strategies as well as help improve global capacity to reduce the number and mitigate the consequences of cyber conflict. The policy and operational consequences of such a multi-stakeholder collaborative defense will require more in-depth research and thought.

Vector Four: Domestic and International Law

One cannot fully grasp the complexity of the emerging dynamics of cyber conflict without a keen appreciation of the domestic and international legal framework for cyber operations. While taking a positivist approach to U.S. and international law, CCSA's research highlights a growing consensus on a number of legal issues. First, the relatively immaturity of applying international and domestic legal constructs to malicious activity in cyberspace has also resulted in a hesitancy of both governmental and private sector actors to take steps to reduce malicious activity that is contributing to the instability of the cyber environment. Additionally, norms and customs related to behavior in cyberspace and obligations for managing cyber conflict must be developed over time. While the process of norm maturation will be potentially difficult and contentious, it is important to begin that dialogue now with both states and non-state actors. Like-minded states must also begin acting on agreed-upon foundations, but the basis for agreement requires broader, more comprehensive thinking about the causes and dynamics of cyber conflict, which can then translate into more-focused regime building efforts and policies. Remaining research issues for the legal and ethical field include exploring the effects of legal norms for cyberspace upon traditional political, social, and economic frameworks. Even more broadly, cyber conflict research must assess the potential contributions of international, regional, and bilateral treaties in governing conflict in cyberspace, especially the interplay between international legal norms and the current attempts to develop policy norms to govern cyber security. Future CCSA research may focus on the maturation of international cyber norms through the implementation of legal regimes and varying models, as norms may play a fundamental role in terms of governance of both state and non-state actors in seeking cyber stability.

Vector Five: Approaches for Mitigating Cyber Conflict

CCSA proposes three approaches for more effective management of cyber conflict challenges. These approaches are not mutually exclusive and may have complementary features regarding their use by the United States and others seeking cyber security. As core assumptions, the models incorporate earlier analysis about cyber instability and the importance of non-state actors, both in their development and their subsequent policy recommendations.

Firstly, the *public health model* considers how useful norms for states and non-state actors, like hygiene, can limit the spread of disease. Furthermore, the mandatory reporting of infectious diseases can provide a model for early warning, prevention, and intervention in cyberspace. The second proposed *environmental model* also focuses on cyber cleanup. It suggests the application of a legal regime to deal with problems such as pollution and provides for a meaningful role for non-state actors, while touching upon similarities with the global development agenda. Finally, *the irregular warfare approach* illustrates how an existing military mindset may be leveraged to provide new insight onto cyber conflict management and mitigation. This approach demonstrates the parallels between the asymmetric and indirect means and tactics employed by irregular warfare and cyber conflict actors. This not to say, however, that our adversaries are engaging in an irregular war in cyberspace—though some may have indeed adopted this as a primary goal/strategy—merely that examining the tactics and strategies of irregular operations on the ground can provide useful insight into conflicts in cyberspace. We believe that the ability to adapt current approaches and think more in terms of management of conflict, as well as developing approaches that prioritize addressing a wide range of actors and the role of collaboration will be essential in informing U.S. policy and meeting the challenges of cyber instability.

The Future of the Cyber Conflict Research Agenda

Each section of this monograph asks new questions or highlights challenges that require more analysis, demonstrating the continued need for innovative, multidisciplinary coordination, and research on cyber conflict.

Regarding strategic-level issues, the posited concept of inherent cyber instability has broad, far-reaching implications for academics, policymakers, and strategists. If decision makers accept that cyberspace is inherently unstable from a strategic conflict management perspective and abandon attempting to create a stable cyber environment, this may naturally result in an increased emphasis on resilience, risk management, and mitigation and the potential creation of risk reduction centers.

There are many important questions about the future of military and intelligence cyber operations, such as: How can the balance of intelligence gain and intelligence loss in cyberspace be better optimized? What research can be conducted into the supply chain dimensions of cyber conflict? How can cyber warfare capabilities be best integrated with other military forces? How can the nation enhance the relationships between and among Department of Defense, Department of Homeland Security, and other key cyber players? How can we find ways to convert research from academia into actionable recommendations for implementation by government?

CCSA research also highlights the critical importance of non-state actors, leading to new questions about their role in cyber conflict: How can we better incorporate the offensive and defensive intent and capability of non-state actors in cyber conflict research? Because the majority of cyberspace is primarily owned, operated, and populated by private actors, what role will they play in cyber conflict? How will the role of the state change vis-à-vis the variety of actors in the cyber ecosystem? What role will non-state actors play in cyber risk reduction?

There is also much important work to be done in the areas of norm development and the ground rules for global collaboration. Future research should explore the boundaries between domestic and international strategy, as well as the different categories for norm development, including the relevant legal, policy, technical, and economic concerns.

While these recommendations may seem daunting when combined, the CCSA cyber conflict research agenda and its further development provides discipline in answering new questions as well as those that have not yet been addressed. One of the key challenges of this field is its interdisciplinary nature, which is reflected in the large number of questions that still remain open for dialogue and discussion.

Closing Call to Action

The Cyber Conflict Studies Association's two-year study has lead to the sobering conclusion that the current strategic cyber environment is fundamentally unstable. What are the implications of this cyber instability? First, it undermines deterrence, especially against non-state actors, who have the significant strategic advantage of being able to limit options for cyber retaliation and may seek to foster an unstable cyber conflict environment. Second, it leads to the temptation to consider preventive war or preemptive war options that would remove the enemy's capacity for effective cyber operations before it can raise its defenses and perhaps even degrade conventional military operations, assuming the adequate intelligence exists to enable effective preemption. Third, it provides strong incentives for escalation to the use of other military capabilities once conflict has begun, primarily to prevent these options from being paralyzed by use of cyber attack. Thus, it is clear that this instability is highly dangerous, especially for status quo cyber actors like the United States who have so much to lose. Indeed, the United States desperately seeks cyber stability for a range of reasons, including continuing economic prosperity, wielding global soft power, and avoiding asymmetric security vulnerabilities with state and non-state adversaries.

Yet despite the hopes and focus of most current approaches to managing cyber security, we cannot expect to achieve cyber stability alone. The U.S. Government has limited influence on the fundamental causes of cyber instability and they look to get worse for an extended period. We cannot construct a safe haven, nor does a cyber high ground exist to seize and hold. Worse, there are difficult tradeoffs in achieving our objectives. Core principles of Internet freedom, tech innovation, and openness/connectivity conflict with the security imperative and our open political system demands that the former be accorded at least equal status with the latter. In response, we must therefore implement a national or even global strategy in cyberspace to create stability through resilience and efforts to clean up the ecosystem. The recent White House strategy is a positive, if belated, move in this direction, but we must acknowledge limits to current approaches and boldly move to claim strategic advantage.

www.ingramcontent.com/pod-product-compliance
Lightning Source LLC
Chambersburg PA
CBHW021852170526
45157CB00006B/2407